FIRST IMPRESSIONS

Peter Paul Rubens

RICHARD MCLANATHAN

Harry N. Abrams, Inc., Publishers

EDITOR: Robert Morton
DESIGNER: Joan Lockhart
PHOTO RESEARCH: Neil Ryder Hoos

LIBRARY OF CONGRESS CATALOGING-IN-PUBLICATION DATA

McLanathan, Richard B. K.
Peter Paul Rubens / Richard McLanathan.
    p.   cm. — (First impressions)
Includes index.
ISBN 0-8109-3780-8 (hc)
1. Rubens, Peter Paul, Sir, 1577–1640—Juvenile literature.
2. Painters—Belgium—Biography—Juvenile literature.
[1. Rubens, Peter Paul, Sir, 1577–1640.   2. Artists.]
I. Title.   II. Series: First impressions (New York, N.Y.)
ND673.R9M38   1995
759.9493—dc20   94-33330

Published in 1995 by Harry N. Abrams, Incorporated, New York
A Times Mirror Company

Printed and bound in Hong Kong

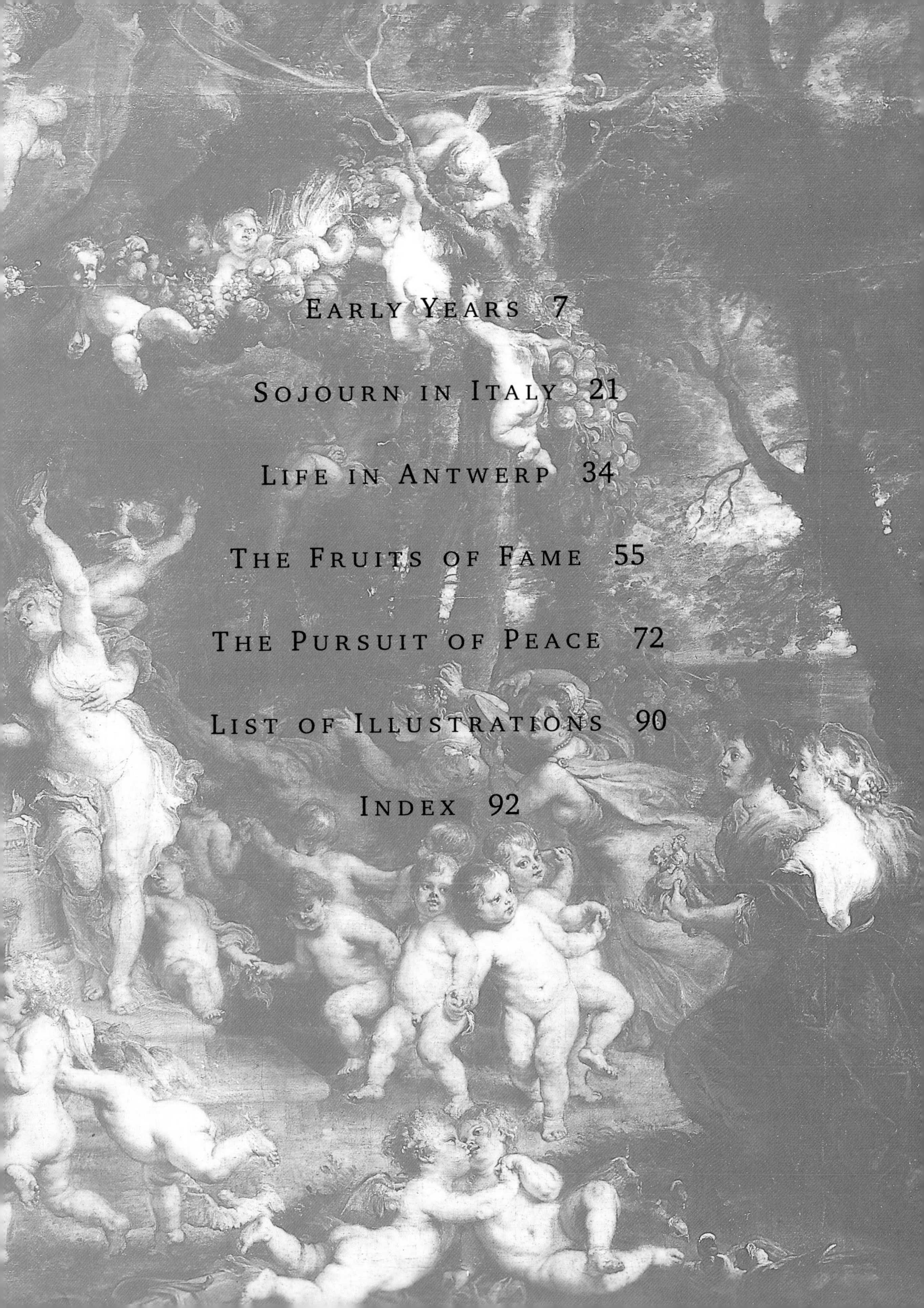

EARLY YEARS

Peter Paul Rubens was born into a distinguished family, whose members had been prominent for centuries in the affairs of their native city of Antwerp. Today Antwerp is in Belgium, but at the time it was part of the Spanish Netherlands, then the possession of the Catholic king of Spain. Jan Rubens, Peter Paul's father, was born a Catholic, as was Maria Pypelinckx, the heiress whom he married. An eminent lawyer, Jan was an alderman of the city.

In those intolerant days one's religion dictated where one lived, so when Jan converted to Calvinism, thus becoming a Protestant, his position in Catholic Antwerp became endangered. In 1568 two distinguished Protestant leaders were executed in Brussels for their faith, and Jan and his family fled to Cologne on the Rhine River in Germany.

Thus it was that Peter Paul Rubens was born in Germany on June 28, 1577, and not in his family's native country. He lived in Germany until he was ten years old, at which time his father died. Maria Rubens then returned to her family in

Rubens practiced his drawing by adding the landscape and other details to this unfinished engraving of St. Jerome in the Wilderness, *thought to be by a member of a family of Flemish engravers, the Sadelers.*

Antwerp with her three children. The eldest was a daughter, Blandina; next came Philip, a teenager; and then Peter Paul. Death had taken the lives of three other children, as so often happened before modern medicine developed.

The Antwerp to which the Rubens family returned was one of the richest and most active seaports in Northern Europe. Its only rival was nearby Amsterdam in the Protestant Netherlands, now Holland.

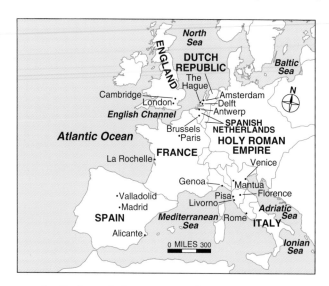

In Rubens' time power in Europe was politically divided between the Bourbons who controlled France and Italy; and the Hapsburgs, who not only ruled Spain but also Germany, Austria, and a combination of smaller states known collectively as the Holy Roman Empire.

Antwerp was located toward the head of the broad gulf where the River Scheldt flows into the North Sea. Goods came overland from Germany to be transshipped throughout the world. The city contained colonies of foreign merchants from Russia, Scandinavia, Portugal, Spain, the British Isles, and the farthest shores of the Mediterranean Sea. It was a center of international banking, where the currencies of the world were exchanged, since the city was a major port of call for ships of all nations, and her own vessels traded with the New World as well as the Old. Most citizens spoke several languages and were used to seeing the exotic costumes of the sea captains and their crews, from furred and bearded Russians to turbaned Turks and colorfully robed Africans.

Like so many cities of the Netherlands, Antwerp had had a difficult history. In

1555 the many provinces of the Netherlands had come by inheritance under the rule of King Philip II of Spain. Annoyed by the stubborn Protestantism that prevailed, especially in the northern section that later became Holland, the Catholic king sent in a Spanish army that devastated the fertile countryside, burning and pillaging. The northern provinces persistently fought back, and, under the leadership of William of Orange, formed the Protestant Dutch Republic, which became a powerful maritime state despite its small size. The southern provinces remained predominantly Catholic, and very gradually, under the rule of more benevolent Spanish royal governors, recovered something of their lost prosperity.

When Maria Rubens and her children returned to Antwerp in 1587, they saw evidence everywhere of the barbarism of the Spanish invaders—burned-out churches, ruined houses, and impoverished inhabitants who had survived the

Antwerp, the great seaport of the Spanish Netherlands, was one of the busiest in Europe.

rioting of ten years before. Then, in four days, more than seven thousand people had been slaughtered in the streets, and the whole center of the city was destroyed. During his early years in Antwerp, Rubens saw the city gradually recover something of its former wealth and dignity, and there seems never to have been any doubt in his mind that he considered Antwerp his home. Also, although he had been baptized a Lutheran, he still considered himself a loyal Catholic.

Though Peter Paul was by nature a happy person with a lively personality and an optimistic disposition, he lived in a deeply troubled world, torn by religious strife. The Protestant Reformation, which had started earlier in the century in which he was born, spread like wildfire throughout Germany, France, and northern Europe, where the corruption and abuses of the Catholic church were perceived as particularly disturbing. The answer of the Church of Rome was to revive the Inquisition, an ecclesiastical court of inquiry that had been established in the Middle Ages to stamp out heresy. In those days there was no such thing as religious freedom. That some people had different ideas from those set forth by the pope was intolerable to the church. Anyone who deviated in any way from official doctrine, and who presumed to interpret the Bible for herself or himself instead of relying solely on the words of a priest, was considered a heretic. Tens of thousands of people were accused of heresy and brought before the courts of the Inquisition, conducted by zealous priests.

The word Inquisition means inquiry, questioning. All too often the questioning took the form of torture, to wring a confession from the accused whether they were guilty or not. The dreadful result was that thousands of men and women were burned at the stake, and countless cities and towns were plundered and destroyed by mercenary armies, whose leaders, ostensibly acting on behalf of the

To learn from the Italian master, Rubens made this copy of Titian's Adam and Eve *in Spain.*

true religion, were actually driven by greed and ambition to gain lands and spoils. Intolerance, superstition, and cruelty pervaded much of Europe during Rubens' lifetime and later, disrupting innumerable lives, and causing unbelievable suffering and misery.

Many loyal Catholics saw the same abuses to which the Protestants objected. As a result, the Counter Reformation was launched from Rome, not only to counteract the growing strength of Protestantism, and to win back adherents to the traditional faith, but also to reform the church from within. So Western Christendom seemed hopelessly divided. Yet the period was also one of great cultural achievement in science as well as in the arts. It produced saints and philosophers whose thoughts and writings changed the course of Western civilization. Rubens was but one, though among the greatest of the artists whose works made the period of the Baroque—the seventeenth and eighteenth centuries—one of the richest in the history of art. Out of the nightmare of bigotry and hate emerged a new spirit expressed in painting, sculpture, architecture, literature, music, and scholarship. The buoyancy of Rubens' own personality matched that aspect of the times in which he lived and to which he so memorably contributed.

The Renaissance, the movement that preceded the era in which Rubens lived, began about 1400 in Florence. During the next century Renaissance ideas spread throughout Italy and then gradually across the rest of Europe. The driving force behind these ideas was the rediscovery of the importance of the individual human being in terms of the arts and thought and creative achievements of ancient Greece and Rome. Scholars searched through the libraries of monasteries where manuscripts of Classical authors had been preserved through the long centuries of the Dark and Middle Ages. The ruins of Classical buildings began to be studied instead of being used as quarries to supply stone for castles and fortresses. Marble statues were preserved instead of being burned for lime to make mortar; they were collected and treasured by popes and princes and used as models by contemporary artists. Greek and Latin became the languages of scholarship and literature, and a knowledge of the authors who spoke and wrote in them was considered essential to a proper education.

This passionate interest in the Classical past was the unifying force that drew together the liveliest minds of Baroque Europe, whatever their religious affiliation. It tempered the prejudices of Catholic and Protestant alike, and it also provided not only a common ground of interest and concern, but also common ideas and ideals that were pursued by the creative minds of the time. Events in Classical history and episodes from the mythology of Greece and Rome formed a shared vocabulary of images used by writers and visual artists alike.

Like his brothers and sisters, Peter Paul had been tutored by his father, and he continued his education in Antwerp in the school of Rombout Verdonck, a much respected scholar. There he studied Greek, Latin, and other languages, history, mathematics, and some science. He came to know an older student, Balthasar Moretus, whose family in 1555 had founded an important printing and publishing business, the Plantin Press. This press, one of the greatest in Europe, was famous for its beautifully produced and edited books on Classical literature as well as philosophical and scientific treatises. Balthasar became a lifelong friend of Rubens

Rubens made the drawing from which Cornelius Galle engraved this title page for a book of poems in Latin written by Pope Urban VIII. The book was printed by the Plantin-Moretus Press.

and was later the director of the press.

Through Verdonck's school and family friends, Rubens met many of the leading citizens of Antwerp. His formal education was soon over, however, because in 1590 his sister Blandina, then in her early twenties, was married. This strained the vastly reduced family fortune because they had to provide a dowry for her, a sum of money traditionally given by the bride's family to help the young couple start their household. As a result, Peter Paul, thirteen years old, and his brother Philip, sixteen, were on their own.

Both boys were mature for their years. Philip had already shown himself to be an unusually capable student, and won employment as secretary to a leading citizen, prominent in the public life of the city. Later he became tutor to his employer's two sons, whom he accompanied to the famous University of Louvain. There he continued his own education, and was soon recognized as an outstanding young scholar of Classical philosophy and literature, and of the early history of the church.

Maria Rubens arranged to have Peter Paul accepted as a member of the household of the Countess of Lalaing, where he perfected the niceties of courtly manners considered essential in the strictly stratified society of the period. Because he came from a privileged background and was bright and quick to learn, there was little that being one of the countess' pages could teach him. The position could well have led to a career in public life, but Rubens already knew that he wanted to be a painter, and he was eager to start. His experience with the countess may not have had much value in preparing him to be an artist, but it undoubtedly did help to equip him for the diplomatic missions that were later to be entrusted to him. It also gave him the self-assurance and the knowledge of protocol, the accepted code of conduct required of courtiers and diplomats, that made it possible for him to maintain an easy association with the aristocratic and royal patrons who were to vie for his attention in later years.

We do not know why Peter Paul Rubens wanted to become an artist. Doing so represented a step down the social ladder in those days. It may have been because a cousin of his mother's had recently married a successful landscape painter named Tobias Verhaecht, whose small pictures were attractive and decorative, and sold well to burghers of Antwerp and to visitors. Verhaecht was typical of many competent minor artists throughout the Low Countries, a number of whom settled in Antwerp which became an increasingly important northern center of art.

It is obvious from looking at his pictures that Verhaecht was properly trained in all the traditional techniques of the professional painter of his time. He had undoubtedly served his apprenticeship with an experienced older artist, and had been taught to grind pigments and to mix them with sun-thickened linseed oil. He had learned to prepare wooden panels and canvases by grounding them with a priming coat to produce a slightly textured surface sympathetic to paint on. He had watched the experienced artist lay in the general structure of his chosen subject in lighter and darker neutral tones, then apply the more transparent, darker colors first, working toward the lighter, then finally paint in the flesh- or sky-tones with a pigment-laden brush. He learned how to clean brushes and to store paints. He was also taught how to prepare a palette, with the paints neatly arranged in small blobs of color around the edge in the particular sequence preferred by the artist, leaving the area in the center for mixing.

There is a natural fascination in the skills involved in all the traditional crafts, like those of the potter working at the wheel to transform a shapeless lump of clay into a useful pot; or those employed by the silversmith to hammer a flat disc of metal into a graceful tea- or coffee-pot. One can imagine that perhaps Rubens saw Verhaecht at work in his studio, surrounded by stretched canvases, supplies of paints, and pots full of brushes, with a painting in process on the easel. As an imaginative boy in his early teens, Peter Paul may well have felt attracted to a painting career through Verhaecht's example. In any event, he soon became an apprentice in Verhaecht's studio.

In all his works one can see the delight that Rubens took in the handling of pigment. It shows in the beautifully ordered, painterly surfaces of his pictures, in the sure and free but controlled brushwork, in the richness and variety of his colors, and in the masterful modulation of textures and surfaces—all express the satisfaction of a superlative craftsman in total control of his medium. But no matter how extraordinary his skills, Rubens was much more than a technician. His craftsmanship, brilliant as it is, is only the means. The human content in his work, the vigor and emotion, the drama, heroism, tragedy, and triumph, the rich symbolism, and, above all, the tremendous energy that pervades everything he did are expressions of a unique and powerful artistic personality. Though he was an outstanding architect, designer, and draftsman, in painting he found his ideal medium.

The Hapsburg prince, Archduke Albert of Austria, and his wife, Isabella, (opposite) were generous patrons of Rubens. He painted these portraits in about 1609.

Rubens did not stay long in Verhaecht's studio. He was very observant and a fast learner, and the range of his master's practice was limited to small decorative landscapes. So he moved on to become an apprentice to a more versatile painter, Adam van Noort, with whom he worked for four years. He then studied briefly with a far more distinguished artist, Otto van Veen, whose reputation had spread far beyond the Netherlands, and who had lived and worked in Rome. In Italy van Veen had seen the works of Michelangelo, Raphael, and other Italian masters of the High

Renaissance when Rome became the world capital of the arts. He had also become deeply interested in symbolism, an aspect of both art and thought that was very popular at the time, and he passed that interest on to Rubens.

Every age has its symbols. Some, like the Christian cross, the Jewish Star of David, and the Moslem star and crescent have continuing meaning. Others, especially those used by yesterday's artists, have been mostly forgotten. Today there is comparatively little use of symbolism in art, because there is no longer a vocabulary of symbols that is widely accepted and understood. We have generally recognized and accepted signs and emblems, however, such as the CBS trademark eye on the television screen, and international city and highway markers. But symbols stand for ideas and imaginative concepts, as well as identifying things and giving nonverbal directions.

In Rubens' time there was a great interest in symbols, which often held clues to the meanings of a painting or sculpture. Saints, for example, had their identifying symbols: St. Catherine's was the wheel because she was tortured "on the wheel" for her Christian faith; St. George's was the dragon; St. Mark, the author of the Gospel of St. Mark in the Bible, was known by a winged lion. Everywhere in Venice one sees the winged lion because St. Mark was the patron saint of the republic. A lion without wings was the symbol of St. Jerome, since, according to legend, while Jerome was fasting in the desert he had removed a thorn from a lion's paw, thus winning the animal's everlasting devotion.

Plant life also provided symbols. A painting of a mother and baby with a sheaf of wheat and a bunch of grapes indicates that the picture is of the Madonna and Child. The grain stands for the bread and the grapes for the wine that is consumed as the body and blood of the Savior during the celebration of the mass, in memory of Christ's sacrifice on the cross.

During the seventeenth century, reference books of symbols and emblems were compiled, identifying the meanings of all sorts of things, from the anchor, standing for hope, to the serpent, often representing wisdom. There were variations, though. When a serpent was shown with a human head, as in old depictions of Adam and Eve about to eat the forbidden apple, it was understood as Satan himself. Classical myths supplied many symbols. Neptune (Poseidon in Greek) with his trident, a three-pronged spear, represents the sea; Minerva (Athena in Greek), with helmet and spear, stands for wisdom and virtue; and Venus (Aphrodite in Greek) personifies love and beauty.

Van Veen had probably brought back from Italy engravings made from the works of leading artists of the Renaissance. Few people could own original paintings, but prints made from engraved copper plates made it possible for almost anyone to have a small-scale black and white version of a painting, whatever its size. Such prints were much collected and could be found in many artists' studios. We know from drawings that Rubens made at this time that he studied through engravings the compositions and details of such masters as Raphael, Titian, and Michelangelo, among many others. We also know that he was fascinated by one of the most famous books of the time, an edition of the Bible printed in Switzerland in 1576 and illustrated with 170 woodcuts designed by a celebrated Swiss artist named Tobias Stimmer. Stimmer's detailed and lively illustrations are full of action and drama, and Rubens mentioned them in later years as a major source of inspiration.

In Otto van Veen, Peter Paul found not only a sympathetic teacher but also a friend. He stayed on in van Veen's studio even after 1598, when he was admitted, at the age of twenty-one, as a master in the Guild of St. Luke, the artists' guild of

Antwerp, and had developed an independent career. Almost nothing is known of his work during these years, but he must have been well regarded or he would not have been invited to submit a painting for approval to the officers of the guild, who elected him a member. We also know that he was busy, and that he had at least one pupil, Deodatus del Monte, the son of a goldsmith.

In the winter of 1599 the new rulers of the Spanish Netherlands, the Archduke Albert von Hapsburg of Austria, and the Archduchess, his cousin Isabella, daughter of Philip II of Spain, arrived in Antwerp. They were welcomed with the kind of elaborate ceremony typical of such events in the period, with trumpets, banners, speeches, bands, parades, and pageantry. With other artists, van Veen and Rubens were involved in designing and painting triumphal arches and other decorations to adorn the route taken by the royal couple, who were called regents. With them were many courtiers and an honor guard of special soldiers assigned to protect them. The event also marked a great change in Peter Paul's life. Early in the year he left for Italy, with his pupil and friend, Deodatus del Monte, because for any Northerner who aspired to a successful artistic career, study in Italy was an essential experience.

Rome was still considered the world capital of the arts, just as it had been during the High Renaissance in the first quarter of the sixteenth century, when Michelangelo and Raphael were enriching the eternal city with their art and architecture. But all the independent states that occupied the Italian peninsula were famous for their artists, from the warlike Duchy of Milan and the prosperous Republic of Venice in the North to the Kingdom of the Two Sicilies in the South, with its capital at Naples, the ancient fortified seaport at the foot of the slopes of the still-smoking volcano, Mount Vesuvius. After about a month's travel on horseback, southeastward through France and Germany, Peter Paul and Deodatus crossed the snowy passes of the Alps, followed down the steep valleys of their southern slopes, and finally descended into Venice.

SOJOURN IN ITALY

Venice was unique among the more powerful states in Italy at that time in maintaining a republican form of government while the rest of the peninsula was dominated by absolutist rulers, whether they were called kings, princes, or dukes. But Venice was not a democracy as we know it. The power to elect the Doge, the city's ruler, lay in the hands of the leaders of a few ancient noble families whose rights were inherited. Its government remained remarkably stable over the centuries, however, through its extraordinary system of checks and balances, of councils and assemblies, and its professional bureaucracy. Its diplomatic service was famous for the accuracy and objectivity of the information supplied to the Doge by ambassadors from all over the world. Its system of spies was notoriously efficient. And its famous navy, consisting of fleets of light, swift galleys, powered by oarsmen and sails, dominated the eastern Mediterranean.

The off-center composition and lively interaction of the figures in this painting by the Venetian master, Titian, greatly influenced Rubens. As was usual at the time, Titian shows portraits of the man who paid for the painting (Jacopo Pesaro, kneeling at the left) and members of his family (behind Jacopo and at the right) in this scene.

When the two Northerners reached Venice, the power of the republic had been in decline for some time. But you would never have known it from the lifestyle of the inhabitants. The crowds in the streets and on the canals were dressed with formal elegance. There were frequent balls, religious processions, and civil ceremonies, many led by the Doge himself, the ruler of the republic, and the councilors, senators, and other state officials, all gorgeously robed in the brilliant costumes appropriate to their rank and office. The theaters and concert halls were full, and there was music everywhere, even on the canals at night, when it was supplied by performers in torch-lit barges and gondolas. The main shopping streets were, as a wondering English traveler of the period reported, "tapestried with cloth of gold, damasks and other silks which the shops expose and hang before their houses. . . . To this add the perfumes, apothecaries' shops, and the innumerable cages of nightingales which they keep, that entertain you with their melody from shop to shop." It seemed as though the carefree elegance of Venetian life increased as the republic's world status grew less.

The other important influence on Rubens among Venetian painters was Tintoretto, who here depicts Moses striking a rock to bring forth water, a miracle told in the Bible.

Venice no longer dominated the Eastern trade. The Portuguese had discovered the sea route to the Orient by sailing around the Cape of Good Hope, up the eastern coast of Africa, and across the Indian Ocean to the Spice Islands, China, and Japan. The Dutch and English soon sent their ships adventuring eastward also. The same year that Peter Paul and his companion reached Venice marked the formation of the London East India Company by a group of English merchants with a charter granted by Queen Elizabeth I. Two years later the Dutch East India Company was formed, and other countries soon followed their lead. As a result, European ports from Stockholm, Copenhagen, London, and Amsterdam in the north to cities of Spain and Portugal, and Genoa and other cities on the Mediterranean shores became rival emporiums of Far Eastern trade. All the spices of the East—pepper, coriander, cinnamon, cloves, ginger, nutmeg, cumin, and mace—became general necessities instead of royal and aristocratic luxuries.

In the meantime, Spanish conquistadors had invaded the native empires of the New World, and slaughtered and enslaved their inhabitants. Galleon after galleon returned to the ports of Spain loaded with stolen riches, gold and gems, to prop up the ramshackle and inefficient dictatorship of the Hapsburg kings, and to finance Spanish armies during the endless religious wars that devastated Europe for decades.

Despite its decline, Venice was still a lively place. It was a particularly happy chance that led Peter Paul first to Venice on his Italian travels, because there he came face-to-face with the works of the two greatest Venetian painters of the sixteenth century, Titian (c. 1488–1576) and Tintoretto (c. 1518–94). The ornate Palace of the Doges is full of their paintings and those of their predecessors, contemporaries, and followers. Peter Paul and Deodatus visited the palace again and again. They also explored the many churches, palaces, and other buildings that contained examples of the work of the leading Venetian artists. As we shall see from the paintings that Rubens made after his Venetian experience, he had studied his great predecessors' achievements to very good effect.

In the summer of 1600, Vincenzo Gonzaga, Duke of Mantua, stopped briefly in Venice on his way home from a trip to northern Europe. He had visited Antwerp, and may there have heard of Rubens as a promising young painter. But, whether

he had already heard of him or not, when a gentleman in his entourage met Peter Paul at the Venetian inn where he was staying, saw some of his work, and reported on it to the duke, Vincenzo offered the young Northerner employment as a court painter. Living as an artist in Italy was not easy in those days. As an established painter with a wide reputation wrote to a friend, "As for commissions! For the past year not a dog has come along to order a picture! . . . I may as well plant my brushes in the garden!" The opportunity provided by Vincenzo Gonzaga was too good to refuse. So in the spring of 1600, Peter Paul set out for Mantua, which is about a hundred and fifty kilometers west of Venice. Mantua is an ancient fortified city, partly bordered by a sweeping curve of the River Mincio, a few miles north of its confluence with the mighty River Po. There the river widens to form three lakes, and to fill the moat of the Castle of St. George, part of the complex of buildings that forms the Ducal Palace.

Vincenzo Gonzaga, the Duke of Mantua, had been brought up to enjoy a court life enlivened by music, masques, and balls in the Ducal Palace, which contains more than four hundred and fifty rooms. The duke continued his family's traditional interest in literature, music, art, and architecture. He entertained a constant stream of distinguished visitors with their followers and servants from all parts of Europe. There were resident poets, artists, and musicians, as well as the famous troup of dwarves for whom the suite of miniature apartments in the palace was especially constructed. The Gonzagas had ruled the duchy since the fourteenth century, and Vincenzo had inherited one of the largest and most notable collections of painting, sculpture, and other objects of art, ancient and contemporary, and was determined to add to it in the most distinguished manner possible.

The duke was affable as well as hospitable, and when he found Peter Paul to

Rubens first drew and then painted the Duke of Lerma on horseback during his visit to Spain on behalf of the Duke of Mantua in 1603.

In 1614 Rubens painted this scene of Joseph and Mary fleeing to Egypt. It seems to have been inspired by a work by his friend Adam Elsheimer.

be a trustworthy young man of taste and tact, he encouraged him to travel where he pleased to make copies of paintings for his collection. As a result, for more than eight years, Rubens was able to explore the artistic wonders of Italy, eagerly studying works of art and architecture of all periods. He had been brought up speaking Italian, and with his attractive personality, easy good manners, and the duke's sponsorship, he managed, as his correspondence with his brother Philip documents, to visit a great many of the finest collections and to meet many of their owners throughout central and northern Italy.

In October 1600 an historically important dynastic marriage took place in Florence. The Medici princess Marie, the younger sister of Vincenzo's duchess, was married to Henry IV, King of France. Henry was so busy trying to settle disturbances in France that he couldn't attend his own wedding, but he was represented by proxy, by the bride's father the Grand Duke of Tuscany. Delegations from almost all the states of Europe were crowded into the cathedral to attend the wedding. Rubens was one of those chosen by Duke Vincenzo to accompany him on the occasion. It was Peter Paul's first meeting with the young queen who was to be-come one of his greatest patrons.

Royal weddings were events of great significance in those days, because they celebrated political alliances of nations as well as of ruling families, so there was much ceremony. Yet Rubens found time to explore the wonders of Florence. He saw the treasures of the Medici collections, and the churches and palaces full of works of art from Classical times to the present. He examined paintings and sculptures by all the greatest Florentines of the Renaissance. He studied Michelangelo's impressive tombs in San Lorenzo, with their immense tragic sculptures of Night and Day, and of Dawn and Dusk, reclining below the seated statues of two Medici princes, brooding in the silence of the funeral chapel.

Rubens spent the winters of 1601–02 in Rome, enjoying, on Duke Vincenzo's recommendation, the patronage of Cardinal Alessandro Montalto, a number of whose paintings he copied for the duke's collection. He also began selling his work to others, as his painting skills became increasingly known among the connoisseurs of the city and many of the visitors who came to Rome from all parts of Europe to study its arts and to patronize its artists. It was at this time that he received his first commission from the Hapsburg rulers of the Spanish Netherlands, with whom he was later to be closely associated. The Archduke Albert ordered three altarpieces for the Roman church of which he was the patron.

Recognizing Peter Paul's unusual diplomatic skills, in the early spring of 1603, the Duke of Mantua sent him off to Spain on a mission, the first of many he was to carry out throughout much of his life. It was a matter of some importance to the duke. The King of Spain was a powerful and very rich monarch who had on more than one occasion meddled in political affairs in Italy, often by sending in troops notorious for their violent behavior, with disastrous results for the local inhabitants. So it was wise policy for the rulers of such small states as Mantua to keep in the Spaniard's good graces. As a special gift the duke sent the King of Spain three pairs of horses, matched in color and size, with a light carriage intricately decorated with Spanish royal insignia and much gilding. Furthermore, it was equipped with the more comfortable system of springs developed by the Italians that proved far superior to the hard-riding, heavy, oversized, rumbling vehicles used by the aristocracy and royalty of most of Europe.

In addition the duke sent examples of the newest refinements in Italian small arms. Their stocks, locks, and barrels were beautifully engraved with mythological subjects appropriate to their lethal purpose. All were highly acceptable gifts for one of the mightiest princes of Europe. Vincenzo also sent to the Duke of Lerma, who was the leading member of the Spanish court and who professed a great interest in the arts, copies of masterpieces of paintings from famous Roman collections.

The journey to Spain was difficult for Peter Paul. The road south from Mantua to Livorno, the major seaport of Tuscany, led across the Apennines, the rugged, mountainous spine of Italy. It was steep and rocky, and the passes were still snowy in the raw March weather. In Livorno the departure of their ship on the month-long voyage to Spain was delayed by bad weather while they awaited clearing and favorable winds. Finally they sailed southwestward, passing Corsica and the Balearic Islands to port, to reach the Spanish Mediterranean seaport of Alicante.

Once in Spain Rubens and his cargo faced a formidable overland journey through the mountains of Murcia and the bare, windy highlands of La Mancha. The sea voyage had been wet and rough, and they had to endure more than three weeks of steady rain on the Spanish leg of their trip. The roads were, if anything, even worse than those they had traversed in Italy. The horses arrived in fine fettle, however, and were washed down with wine to ready them for presentation to the king. But when the paintings were unpacked, Rubens discovered that the rain had soaked through their layers of wrapping. He dried them out and touched them up as needed, but found two so completely damaged that they were beyond repair. He quickly painted a large canvas of his own to replace one of the lost works, much to the admiration of the Spaniards. The Duke of Lerma was so pleased with his gift of paintings, which he seems to have considered originals instead of copies (Peter Paul was too diplomatic to correct the impression), that he ordered a life-sized portrait of himself on horseback.

In Rubens' portrait he deliberately chose a low viewpoint, so the duke's horse looms imposingly tall as it moves toward the spectator at a lively pace, caught by the painter in mid-stride. The rider's easy seat and the jaunty and distinguished air with which he controls the mettlesome animal express the duke's position not only as commander of the king's cavalry, but also as prime minister and a dominant personality in the royal court. The Lerma painting became the model for a long series of equestrian portraits, and

Elsheimer's version of the same subject painted about 1610, also takes place in a magical moonlight landscape.

so pleased the court that the news of Rubens' success soon traveled far beyond Spain even before his own return to Italy.

In the meantime, he enjoyed the favor of the king and his courtiers, and took advantage of the opportunity to study and make copies of a number of the masterpieces in the famous royal collection. He endured with dignity and grace the suffocating formalities of the Spanish court, with its ritualized code of behavior and elaborate rules of precedence and privilege based upon the degree of nobility of those allowed to approach the monarch. His unfailing good manners and his intelligence won the approval of Philip III. In the process he also earned the gratitude of the Duke of Mantua for his diplomatic skill, and achieved the promising beginning of an international reputation, all at the age of twenty-six.

Italian painter Caravaggio shocked many by using the faces of ordinary street people rather than idealized figures. His use of dramatic contrasts of light and dark influenced Rubens, Rembrandt, and many others.

Peter Paul found that his reputation had preceded him when, in 1604, he stopped at Genoa on his way back to Mantua. There Nicolo Pallavicini, Duke Vincenzo's banker and a prominent citizen, introduced him to many of the city's leading families. He received a number of commissions for portraits and orders for altarpieces. Thereafter he included a number of Genoese patricians among his most admiring patrons. He was so impressed with the handsome palaces of the nobility that he made drawings of many of them, measured and reproduced to scale, like architects' designs. Some years later, in 1621, he published a

The powerful illusionism of Guilio Romano's Fall of the Giants, *which Rubens had seen in Mantua, inspired the artist when he was asked by the Spanish king for a series of paintings to decorate a hunting lodge near Madrid.*

splendid book, *Palazzi di Genova*, generously illustrated with engraved plans, cross-sections, and elevations. These were executed with such accuracy that they could serve as a source for anyone who wished to build a house in the best Italian taste.

In 1605, back in Mantua, Rubens received and completed the only order of any importance that the duke ever gave him. It was for three large paintings for the church of the Most Holy Trinity—*The Baptism of Christ, The Gonzaga Family Adoring the Trinity,* and *The Transfiguration.* (Only the second is still in Mantua, now in the Ducal Palace, the others having been sold to pay the duke's debts.) The artist was in such high favor with the duke that he was allowed to go to Rome for an extended stay. There he and his brother Philip lived on the Via della Croce, not far from the Spanish Steps. Philip was serving as librarian to Cardinal Ascanio Colonna, a position that provided an excellent opportunity to continue the Classical research he had begun while studying with Justus Lipsius at the University of Louvain. Peter Paul shared his brother's interests, and for two years they explored the ruins and relics of ancient Rome.

While Philip gathered material for a book on the patterns of life of the Classical Romans, Peter Paul made drawings from sculptures showing their costumes, customs, and religious rituals, sacrifices, and processions. These drawings were the originals of the engravings that illustrated Philip's book, which was published in Antwerp by their friend Balthasar Moretus, director of the Plantin Press.

In 1607 Philip returned to Antwerp, leaving his brother in Rome to continue his study of painting, sculpture, and architecture. He also produced portraits and altarpieces for several Genoese patrons. Officially Peter Paul remained in the service of the Duke of Mantua, but his salary was often not paid because of the duke's financial troubles. Then, in the fall of 1608 his Italian career was abruptly cut short by the news from his brother in Antwerp that his mother was gravely ill.

Peter Paul departed at once on the long trip north across the Alps to the Netherlands. He left word with the duke's steward that he was leaving, but planned to return soon. He saw his future in Italy, which he regarded as his spiritual home. He had no idea that he would never again be there except for visits, and that his future lay, neither in Mantua nor in Rome, but in all of Europe.

Rubens' Italian experience had been invaluable. It had made it possible for him to absorb the spirit and the attitudes of Italian life, so different from those of the North, where he had been born. It enabled him to explore that other dimension of the Mediterranean world that meant as much to him as to his brother, the echoes and remains of the Classical past. Also, instead of being able to study only engravings and copies of the works of his great predecessors, like Titian, Tintoretto, Raphael, and Michelangelo, he had been surrounded by their original works in galleries, churches, and palaces. He had walked the streets where they had walked, had viewed the scenes of their everyday lives, and discussed their methods and their achievements with others who shared his enthusiasm.

Peter Paul had also discovered many contemporary artists of whom he would scarcely have been aware if he had stayed in the North. Among those who were especially interesting to him was the shy and hesitant Adam Elsheimer, a German who lived in Rome, and Caravaggio, a reckless and headstrong Italian. Elsheimer's small, mysterious landscapes, often moonlit, he found fascinating. Caravaggio's violent use of contrasting lights and darks, intensely theatrical interpretation of his subjects, and choice of street people as models for Biblical characters shocked most viewers, but gave Rubens much food for thought.

All the memories of his life in Italy remained vividly with him—the sculpturesque frescoes by Mantegna in the Ducal Palace in Mantua, the immense struggles of Giants and Titans by Giulio Romano on the walls of the Palazzo del Te nearby, Raphael's frescoes in the Vatican, and Michelangelo's in the Sistine Chapel. All this rich Italian experience became a vital part of himself and confirmed a heroic view of life that can be seen in all his works, from sketches to mural paintings and architectural designs. He had left much of himself in Italy as well, in the altarpieces in Mantua, Genoa, and Rome, and the opulent portraits, all of which became models for artists of succeeding generations, who recognized him as the peer of the great masters whom he so admired.

LIFE IN ANTWERP

T hough he traveled as fast as he could, Peter Paul arrived in Antwerp too late to see his mother alive. However, he had brought with him from Rome a large altarpiece that he considered the finest painting that he had yet done. This became her memorial.

Other family news was happier. Before his mother's final illness, his brother Philip had become engaged and a wedding date had been set. Peter Paul was much involved with the arrangements for the ceremony that took place in the early spring of 1609. He was also invited by Archduke Albert and Archduchess Isabella to enter their service. "Their offers are very generous," he wrote a friend in Rome, though "I have little desire to become a courtier again." But his natural patriotism won out. After all, the archduke had given him his first important commission. Furthermore, Albert and Isabella had proved themselves serious and dedicated rulers who did all they could to rebuild the prosperity that had prevailed before the disastrous Spanish armed intervention had plunged the country into an enduring depression during the last quarter of the previous century.

In 1609 a twelve-year truce was finally arranged between the Protestant Netherlands to the north and the Catholic Spanish Netherlands to the south. The prospect of peace, even of limited duration, was welcome after almost a half-century of war. Trade was gradually resumed, and the wharves along the southern bank of the Scheldt became busy again. An increasing number of vessels made

35

About 1611 Rubens painted The Raising of the Cross, *the first of two immense altarpieces he created for Antwerp's cathedral.*

Between 1611 and 1614 Rubens completed his second work for the cathedral, the central panel of which shows Christ's body being lowered from the cross. The side panels show early scenes from the story of Christ's life. The left wing of the triptych depicts the Virgin Mary meeting with Elizabeth; the right wing records the Presentation in the Temple.

their way to Antwerp up the long estuary from the North Sea. The churches and other buildings that had been burned out during the rioting of the mutinous Spanish troops in the fall of 1576 began to be rebuilt and restored. Life once again resumed some part of the ease of the happy years before the Spanish invasion.

Increasingly Rubens found himself at home in Antwerp. He had many friends there, especially among the large group of artists whose presence and activities made the city one of the leading artistic centers of northern Europe. More persuasive still was a charming young woman named Isabella Brant. She was a niece of Philip's wife, and the daughter of one of Rubens' older friends, the distinguished scholar Jan Brant. Peter Paul had seen a great deal of her during the period leading up to his brother's wedding. During the summer of 1609 he found himself completely in love with Isabella. When she assured him that she returned his affection, a new chapter in his life began. Early in the fall he accepted the regents' offer to become the official artist to their court in Brussels, though he was not required to live there, and he and Isabella were married.

To commemorate his wedding, Rubens painted a double portrait of Isabella and himself seated in a bower of honeysuckle. There had been many portraits painted to celebrate newly married couples, but none up to this time had been as studiously casual as this one. Though the handsome young pair are dressed with great elegance, their poses are comfortable and informal, each leaning toward the other, their hands joined. The bride is a picture of the high fashion of the day, from her cameo bracelets to a crisply starched ruff and a delightfully absurd tall hat with artfully folded brim. Her plum-colored silk skirt flows onto the grass in shimmering liquid ripples. Both figures are relaxed and look out at us with a direct gaze that contrasts sharply with the almost frivolously chic costumes. They are a beguilingly attractive pair, and their marriage turned out to be as ideal as all marriages are supposed to be but seldom are.

Two years after Peter Paul and Isabella were married, he bought a house, a tall, handsome structure of brick with stone trim that had considerable land around it. It was almost a century old when Peter Paul acquired it. It had been designed in a classic Netherlandish style, with high, beamed ceilings and cavernous fireplaces with cast-iron fire-backs and sides inset with colored tiles. Sculptured brackets supported head-high mantelpieces. The rooms were lighted by many-tiered chandeliers and candlesticks of gleaming brass. The walls were hung with tapestries or leather, tooled in gilded patterns in the Spanish fashion, and paintings, many of them portraits, framed in dark wood striped with gold. There were colorful Oriental rugs on the floors, which were paved in geometrical patterns of contrasting light and dark squares of polished stone.

The rooms were large and comfortable and were furnished with chairs in the Netherlandish style with turned wooden legs and rungs, backs and seats upholstered in leather or with embroidered cloth, sturdy tables with spiral-turned legs, and tall cabinets in dark wood with paneled doors. The beds were large and canopied, with curtains that could be drawn so that at night they became private little rooms shielded against the damp chill of the nearby sea. It was an appropriate house for a family of taste, wealth, and established social position.

The gardens were laid out in a formal design, with clipped hedges and terraces, balustrades, urns, a central fountain, and a decorative summer house emphasizing the main axis. Close to the house, and attached to it by a covered walk in the form of a triumphal arch adorned with statues, Rubens constructed a two-storied studio. He designed it in the style he so admired in Italy, complete with Classical sculptures, panels carved in relief with mythological subjects, and elaborately sculptured architectural details, all carried out in stone.

In the studio he displayed the extraordinary collection that he had acquired, mostly in Italy, and to which he kept adding throughout much of his life. There were paintings, drawings, and prints; a large cabinet of antique coins, medals, and gems; sculptured figures and busts, and small bronzes, both Classical and Renaissance; and examples of the elaborate goldsmith work whose craftsmanship he so admired. In the studio he entertained patrons and the procession of aristocratic and royal visitors who were attracted by the fame of the artist and his unique collections.

In 1609 Rubens celebrated his marriage to Isabella Brant with this double portrait.

Probably as a tribute to his dead brother Philip, Rubens painted
Four Philosophers, *showing (from the right) Jan Woverius, Justus Lipsius*
(Philip's teacher), Philip Rubens, and Peter Paul himself. The bust is of the
Roman Stoic philosopher, Seneca.

After his return to Antwerp, Rubens kept in touch by letter with friends in Italy and elsewhere. He wrote easily and well in several languages, though he seems to have preferred Italian, and kept up a lively correspondence. In the winter of 1611 he received word from Rome that his old friend, Adam Elsheimer, had died at thirty-two, leaving his family impoverished. Rubens wrote at once to Elsheimer's young widow, a Scottish woman he had married five years before, offering to help her sell the paintings that remained in her husband's studio to relieve the family's poverty. Elsheimer had been a shy and sensitive man who was heartlessly imposed upon by creditors because of debts incurred during bouts of depression when he was unable to work. As Rubens wrote to a mutual friend, "if the paintings should not be sold immediately, we shall in the meantime find a way to advance her a good sum of money . . . without prejudice to the sale." He lamented that Elsheimer's melancholia had "deprived the world of most beautiful things," and finally reduced him to despair.

Rubens' estimate of his friend's art has been borne out by time. Elsheimer's rare paintings, all small and, in the northern fashion, painted on copper panels, are much prized today. They had a strong influence, not only on Rubens, but also on leading artists of the succeeding generation, among them the great French classical landscapist, Claude Lorraine, and most emphatically on Rembrandt himself. Elsheimer's untimely death caused Rubens great sadness. It cut painfully short an artistic career of remarkable promise, and suddenly deprived him of an imaginative and sympathetic friend.

Another, and much more personal, loss occurred in midsummer of the same fateful year. Abruptly, without warning, and totally unexpectedly, his much loved brother Philip died. He was only thirty-eight, and left his young wife pregnant with a son who was born just two weeks after his father's death. He and his brother had been very close all their lives. Philip had been a favorite companion as well as his nearest sibling. Peter Paul was devastated.

Within a year or so of Philip's death, Rubens began a painting, conceived in large part as a memorial to his brother, of a group of leading scholars and philosophers of his generation. It shows four men, three of whom are seated around a table that is covered, as was often the case in those days, with a colorful Turkish carpet on which are several leather-bound volumes, quill pens, and an inkwell. The dominant figure, second from the right, is the illustrious scholar, Justus Lipsius, whose expressive hand gesture relates him to Philip, his pupil, seated at his master's right. Philip has a pen in his hand to suggest his authorship. To Lipsius' left, our right, is Jan Woverius, in profile, his dog at his knee. His intellectual interests are symbolized by the open book that he holds. Peter Paul himself stands in front of the red drapery to the far left.

The title of the painting, *The Four Philosophers,* refers to those seated around the table and to Seneca, the famous Roman philosopher, a bust of whom occupies a niche above Woverius' head. Seneca was an exponent of Stoicism, a school of philosophy that stood for the control by reason, rather than by emotion, of human behavior, a belief shared by Lipsius and his companions. The tulips in a glass vase

In 1610, when Rubens bought this handsome Antwerp house in the traditional Flemish style, it was already about a hundred years old. He added a two-story studio in the Italian Baroque manner, which is attached to the house by an arcade. Opposite is a room set up for dining as it might have been in Rubens's time.

placed beside the bust in the niche show the group's admiration for him. Rubens included the portrait of himself as his brother's collaborator and as the creator of this painted tribute to him and the others.

At his death, Philip had left in manuscript a translation of the writings of a now totally forgotten churchman of the fifth century, St. Asterius, a bishop once famous for the effectiveness of his preaching. Balthasar Moretus, a schoolfriend of the brothers who had become director of the Plantin Press, which had printed the book on which they had collaborated, published the manuscript as a memorial to

Philip. The handsome volume contains a brief biographical essay on the author by Jan Brant, Isabella's father, and as a frontispiece a portrait of Philip engraved after a drawing by Peter Paul. So Philip's book was an appropriate memorial to him and what he had achieved during his short life.

The Plantin Press, established by Christophe Plantin, Balthasar Moretus' grandfather, was the largest in Europe, with 120 craftsmen manning twenty presses. It printed books in many languages that were universally admired for their scholarship, design, and typography. They were acquired by libraries and individuals across the Continent and beyond. Peter Paul's connection with the press continued throughout most of his career. He developed the ideas for illustrations they required and produced the finished drawings, tailored with great skill to the demands of the expert engravers employed by the press. In this way he created numbers of title pages and illustrations, that, in turn, became the source of ideas and inspiration for countless other artists and designers for years to come.

Rubens had great respect for the effectiveness of engravings in giving broad currency to his compositions and visual ideas, and he employed only the most skilled and knowledgeable craftsmen to reproduce his work. The engraver translated the drawings into lines cut into a copper plate with a sharp steel instrument called a graver. When the plate was inked and wiped the incised lines retained the ink so that, under pressure, the design could be printed on a sheet of paper. Produced in multiple, the engravings were sold in print shops, by booksellers, and by peddlers. They were inexpensive and popular, and did much to spread his fame and influence. Furthermore, their sale afforded him considerable income as well as bringing him additional patrons.

In 1610 Rubens completed the first of the two great altarpieces that established his preeminence among Netherlandish painters. It was commissioned for the church of St. Walpurgis and is now in the north transept of the cathedral of Antwerp, the largest church in Belgium. It is a vast triptych with the central panel showing the *Elevation of the Cross.* The subject is interpreted with intense drama.

The figure of the crucified Christ forms a bold diagonal extending from the lower right back in space toward the upper left, creating an illusion of great depth. The straining figures of the men striving to lift the heavy cross into position add both to the tragedy and tension of the scene, as do the contrast of light and shade and the agitated barking of the superbly painted dog at lower left.

The left-hand wing shows the Virgin and St. John with other grief-stricken mourners, and the one to the right is occupied by a group of Roman soldiers commanded by a bearded officer mounted on a dappled horse. The triptych is fifteen feet high by twenty-four feet across when the wings are open, so the actors in the drama are larger than life-size. The combination of color and form expressed with highlighted figures and details seen against the dark shadows of the rough setting raises the theatrical power of the scene to an almost painful pitch.

The second of the two altarpieces occupies a similar position in the opposite transept of the cathedral. It is a *Descent from the Cross* painted from about 1611 to 1614. It serves as a pendant to the first, which shows the raising of the cross with the living Christ about to make His sacrifice for humankind. The *Descent* commemorates the completion of this phase of the Biblical prophecy with the removal of His dead body, the sacrifice having been completed. It is called the Altar of the Crossbowmen because it was commissioned and paid for by a religious confraternity of laymen devoted to the church and the protection of the city. It is also a very large triptych, with the central panel showing Joseph of Arimathea, Nicodemus, and their companions devoutly lowering the dead body of Christ from the cross, tenderly assisted by a red-robed St. John to the right, the Virgin to the left, and, below, St. Mary Magdalene. There is no tension here, only profound sorrow and infinite respect. The wings are similarly without violence. That to the left depicts the Biblical episode known as the Visitation, when the Virgin greets the elderly Elizabeth, both women miraculously pregnant, Mary with the infant Christ, and Elizabeth with the child who was to become St. John the Baptist, who came out of the desert to herald Christ's ministry and baptize Him in the waters of the River Jordan. The right-hand wing of the altarpiece illus-

In one of the most dramatic Greek myths, Zeus, king
of the gods, orders Prometheus chained to a rock to have his
liver pecked out by an eagle because he gave the sacred
gift of fire to mankind. Rubens' frequent collaborator
Franz Snyders, painted the ferocious eagle.

trates the Presentation in the Temple, another gentle and undramatic subject.

The entire triptych is painted in the rich, colorful tonalities Rubens learned in Venice, and is composed with a greater unity on a grander scale than is the case with the earlier triptych. Since producing the agonized *Elevation of the Cross,* he had gained in maturity and he created in the *Deposition* a work that soon came to be admired far and wide. It established his position not just as the leading Flemish artist, but also as the foremost painter of his generation in Europe.

In such paintings as these Rubens was developing his mature style, a style based on a masterful orchestration of figures in space, in compositions full of movement and emotion, painted in glowing colors, ranging in tone from brilliant highlights to deepest shadow. It became the dominant style for two centuries, the style known throughout Europe and Latin America, where it was taken by the Spanish and Portuguese colonizers, as the Baroque.

The word Baroque, *barocco* in Italian, originally meant "irregular," and seems first to have been applied to irregularly shaped pearls, meaning flawed or imperfect. The word is thought to have been used first to characterize the art of the seventeenth century in an unflattering way, because of its radical departure from the classicism of the previous period, the Renaissance. Like the term Gothic, which originally meant barbaric, Baroque came to be the accepted name for the style of its period, without any negative implication.

Rubens was a leader in the creation of this spirited and robust style, whose vitality continued throughout the rest of his own century, and, with some changes, well into the next. It prevailed in all the arts—in sculpture, architecture, the theater, and music, as well as in painting and graphic arts. It is a style that suited and expressed Rubens' temperament in its vigor, straightforward demonstration of feeling, and whole-hearted participation in life. It could convey his genuinely devout piety as well as his love for his family, whose members often served as his models. It expressed his sense of the heroic in history, mythology, and scripture, his empathic awareness of the beauty of life, and his intense interest in the natural world and its diverse inhabitants.

FRUITS OF FAME

From about 1610, when he was planning and painting the two great altarpieces that established his reputation, Rubens began also to create the battle and hunting scenes that delighted so many of his royal and aristocratic patrons. Both the Bible and Classical mythology supply an infinite number of dramatic subjects which he illustrated in a series of canvases. One of these was the *Defeat of King Sennacherib* before the walls of Jerusalem by a heavenly host. The actual event seems to have taken place in 401 B.C., but Rubens' composition reflects the account in the second Book of Kings in the Old Testament. Warrior angels dive headlong at the terrified Assyrian army from a midnight sky, whose black clouds are rent by shafts of golden light to reveal the rout of the invading troops as they flee the wrath of heaven.

About 1516 Peter Paul received a commission from Maximilian, Duke of Bavaria, for four hunting scenes that provided an opportunity to show his mastery of animal form and his extraordinary ability to depict exotic beasts in violent action. The paintings show huntsmen, both mounted on horseback and afoot, in dramatic confrontation with lions, tigers, leopards, crocodiles, rhinoceroses, hip-

(previous page) *In the* Defeat of King Sennacherib *Rubens added great drama to the brief biblical account by showing warrior angels plunging from the night sky to rout the terrified Assyrian army and save Jerusalem from capture.*

Rubens painted a number of savage and dramatic hunting scenes as palace decorations for European aristocracy and royalty.

popotamuses, and other animals. There are tangled masses of struggling figures, fierce hunting dogs, rearing horses, thrusting lances, and swinging swords in a wild melee of terrifying ferocity. The effect is heightened by the observer's view-

point, which is so low that the fallen and wounded hunters and the dead and dying animals are at eye level, with the center of the action looming above, threateningly close. The animals are painted with a powerful authority, and have a fierce nobility as they fight for their lives that is in marked contrast to the brutish muscularity of the hunters.

Though everything is depicted with the greatest naturalism, the scenes are completely unreal, and Rubens' patrons understood this perfectly well. They are dramatic entertainments, variations on the theme of the hunt, and reminders that it had long been the prerogative of aristocracy and royalty to display their prowess by slaughtering wild animals. It is a tradition as old as history. But by Rubens' time the tradition was carried on in more modest hunts of game birds, deer, or foxes. Nevertheless in such paintings as these, commissioned as sumptuous palace decorations, there was a picturesque continuation of the same ancient tradition.

Rubens made this drawing of a lioness in preparation for his painting of Daniel in the Lions' Den.

Peter Paul had ample opportunity to study exotic animals from life because Europe's rich and powerful had kept collections of them in private zoos since medieval times. Lions, tigers, elephants, giraffes, and other non-European species were valued diplomatic gifts from one ruler to another. Possession and display of them were symbolic of the authority and high position of their owners.

Rubens was able to achieve these dramatic works because he studied not only from nature, but also the arts of other periods as well as of his own times. Especially in Italy, he explored works of the Classical past. In a Latin essay "On the Imitation of Statues," he wrote that "to achieve . . . the highest degree of perfection in painting, one should, I am convinced, know the works of art of antiquity intimately and be deeply versed in their understanding." The powerful physique of many of his male figures, such as those of the hunters, for example, reflects his admiration for the famous Belvedere torso in the collection of the Vatican, a fragment of the Roman past that strongly influenced Michelangelo. He also borrowed details from a late Classical sculptural group also in the Vatican. Rediscovered in 1506 during the Renaissance, it shows Laocöon, a priest of Apollo, and his two sons struggling with terrifying serpents sent by the vengeful god to devour them because Laocöon had broken his priestly vows.

In Florence Peter Paul so admired Leonardo da Vinci's preliminary drawing for his uncompleted mural painting in the Palazzo della Signoria, the seat of the Florentine government, that he made a spirited copy of it, now in the Louvre in Paris. It shows an episode from the *Battle of Anghiari*, a wild cavalry engagement. In this extraordinary work, dating from 1503, Leonardo anticipated the Baroque style that Rubens perfected more than a century later. Its direct influence on the latter's creative imagination can be seen in the spiraling action of the mounted men, the same compositional principle that governs Rubens' battle and hunt scenes, and his renditions of other subjects as well.

Unlike other painters who also studied the arts of the past, Rubens made all the various elements entirely his own. His compositions are never mere collections of borrowings. They are cohesive, intricately orchestrated expressions of his own energetic spirit. All the rich array of elements that fascinated him, from details of Classical statues, poses from Michelangelo's painting and sculpture, and figures from Raphael, to the dynamics of motion from Leonardo and the color of Venice, are assimilated to his own vigorous and inimitable style.

The unifying principle for Rubens was his own view of nature and the world. He had stored in his imagination the visual experience of what he had seen, from the bleak, windswept highlands of Spain and the rugged slopes and peaks of the

In 1506 this Greek sculpture of Laocoön and his sons was dug up in Rome. The violent emotionalism of the struggling figures influenced Michelangelo and many later artists, including Rubens.

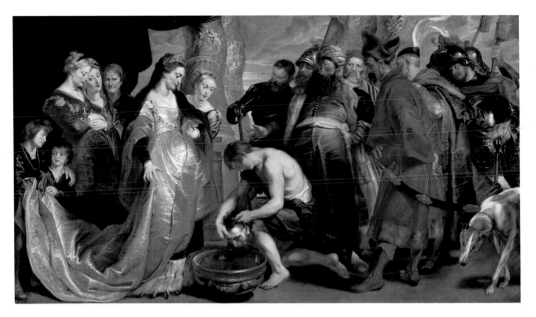

In this scene from ancient history, Rubens used his own two sons,
Nicholas and Albert, as models for the queen's train-bearers. The boar
hound to the right, a Rubens family pet, was probably painted
by Franz Snyders.

Alps and of Italy's Apennines, to the haunted, empty countryside around Rome, with its fragments of ancient aqueducts and tombs, and the endless extent of the flat, fertile, low-lying fields of the Netherlands. But he also vividly remembered the feelings and sensations with which he experienced them, and, above all, the people who inhabited them. It was the essentially human-centered attitude with which he experienced everything in life that provided the common denominator to his work, whether expressing heroism and beauty, misfortune and tragedy, or history or myth.

Rubens' position as court painter to the Hapsburg rulers of the Spanish Netherlands, the Archduke Albert and the Archduchess Isabella, who were understanding and supportive patrons, gave him an ideal base from which to work. Their trust and friendship led to an active diplomatic career that made him unique among the artists of his time, and also broadened the sources of his patronage. He enjoyed another distinct advantage enjoyed by few other artists: he was born a gentleman. In a profoundly class-conscious age, his birth opened doors to him that were totally closed to most. His knowledge of the elaborate rituals of the royal courts, his command of half a dozen languages, and his tact encouraged the royal governors to entrust him with missions of increasing delicacy and importance.

Europe badly needed such skilled diplomats. It was divided between Protestant and Catholic powers. Spain was determined to Catholicize the continent by force if necessary, and the situation was so unstable that it was bound eventually to explode. The fuse was lit in 1618, when a group of Protestants from Bohemia, angered by the revocation of the royal charter that allowed them free exercise of their religion, threw the two Catholic governors out of a second-story window in the royal palace in Prague. They landed in a ditch seventy feet below, bruised but otherwise uninjured except in their pride. This violent and colorful event, which came to be dignified by historians as "the Defenestration of Prague," triggered the horrors of the Thirty Years' War. This war, which lasted for the rest of Rubens' lifetime and beyond, came to an end only in 1648. Exhausted by the endless destruction, the European powers agreed at the Treaty of Westphalia to recognize the right to exist of the various Protestant states, such as the Dutch Republic. The continent was still divided, but people were no longer at one another's throats.

It was against this background of a war-torn Europe that Rubens lived his artistic life, and to the resolution of these conflicts he devoted his diplomatic talents. In the pursuit of peace he traveled tirelessly, to Spain, to England, to Paris, and elsewhere, but always carrying on his active artistic career.

During the years after his return from Italy to Antwerp, Peter Paul had been developing a large studio with a small group of expert assistants and a number of students selected from among the dozens he was requested by friends and patrons to instruct. Among his special assistants were such distinguished artists as the landscapist and flower painter, Jan Brueghel, son of the great recorder of Flemish peasant life, Pieter Brueghel the Elder; Jan Snyders, the celebrated painter of animals; and Anthony van Dyck, who started out as a Rubens pupil, became his chief assistant, and later, as court painter to the King of England, was recognized as one of the greatest portrait painters of all time.

Though Europe was torn by tension and discord, Peter Paul's home and studio were havens of peace and cooperation. Because of the variety and depth of skills among his assistants and students, Rubens could take on one large commission after another and still have time for his family and other activities. He made numbers of small sketches as models for the subjects to be completed, often at mural size. These sketches were extremely swiftly done, with extraordinary freedom and flair, on small, prepared wooden panels, which he preferred for such things, reserving stretched canvas for his larger paintings. He produced no frescoes— paintings on wet plaster—the classic mural medium of the Renaissance. Instead, for mural commissions, he had canvases prepared to fit the shape and dimensions of the desired wall- or ceiling-spaces, and executed them in oil, the technique of the great Venetians whom he so admired.

Unlike most artists of his time, Rubens scrupulously informed his patrons who had prepared the products of his studio. In a letter, dated April, 1618, to Sir Dudley Carleton, a prominent member of the British court, for example, he included a list of the paintings that he thought Sir Dudley would be interested in acquiring for his own collection. In each case he specified whether the painting was "an original, by my own hand," or "begun by one of my pupils, after a picture painted by me, . . . but entirely retouched by my hand."

Among other paintings that Rubens offered to the Englishman he listed a "Christ crucified, in life-size, estimated as perhaps the best painting ever done by me." This is the picture now in the Museum of Fine Arts in Antwerp, known as the *Coup de Lance* from the fact that it shows Longinus, the Roman centurion, piercing Christ's side with his spear. The calmness of Christ's body is in marked contrast to the agonized contortions of the two thieves who have been crucified on either side of Him. The sorrowing Mary Magdalene raises a hand in protest, and St. John and the Virgin recoil at the gratuitous cruelty of the act. But Christ feels no pain because His spirit has already departed.

The *Coup de Lance* was painted in 1620, the year that a small group of determined English Protestants embarked in an overcrowded little merchantman on a long and stormy passage across the Atlantic, to land at Plymouth in what is now the state of Massachusetts. Refugees from the intolerance and violence of seventeenth-century Europe, they faced the "howling wilderness" of the New World, a startling contrast to the formality and courtly ritual of the Old World in which Rubens lived and worked. Almost all of Europe was totally unaware of this small

In 1617 Rubens painted six large canvases for a patron in Genoa as designs for tapestries. They illustrate the life of an ancient Roman hero, Decius Mus, who, as shown in this last scene, died victoriously in battle.

In 1621 Rubens was asked by Marie de' Medici to paint twenty-one large canvases commemorating her life. This portrays her marriage to Henry IV of France, who could not be present at the wedding; standing in for him is Marie's father, the Grand Duke of Tuscany.

event that only later was to be recognized as a more important landmark in history than all the bloody battles of the Thirty Years' War.

With his large studio and group of expert assistants, Rubens was well prepared to undertake the extensive decorative schemes appropriate for the vast scale of Baroque palaces and churches. These schemes consisted of both paintings and tapestries. Large, woven textile wall hangings, tapestry was a craft tradition dating from the Middle Ages, especially in royal factories in Brussels and Paris. In 1617 a group of Genoese patrons ordered from Rubens a suite of six tapestry designs illustrating the career of the ancient Roman consul and general, Decius Mus. Rubens' job was to paint six large canvases that would serve as models for the highly skilled weavers. Consulting the works of the Roman historian Livy, Peter Paul selected six episodes that appealed to his imagination, and depicted them in six immense paintings. The final scene he chose was of the tumultuous battle that ended in victory for the Romans, but cost the heroic warrior his life.

In 1622 the young French king, Louis XIII, requested Rubens to design another tapestry series. There were to be twelve scenes this time, to illustrate the life of Constantine, the Roman emperor who first established Christianity as the religion of the empire in the fourth century.

Reproducing sketches and paintings in tapestry is an exceedingly complicated process. All the colors, the modeling, shading, and details of the artist's designs must be translated into a totally different medium. The weavers must choose and use threads and yarns of many shades to fashion a single, hand-woven fabric, often many square yards in size. The looms were immense, and several extremely skilled and experienced workers toiled at each, most having been brought up in the craft since childhood. It often took years to produce series such as these, so they were affordable by only the richest and most powerful. But, since more than one set of tapestries could be produced from a single series of designs, they were a favorite form of mural decoration among European royalty and aristocracy. Furthermore, they added a welcome sense of ease and even of warmth, though perhaps only visually, to the endless drafty corridors and lofty halls and chambers of masonry buildings whose only sources of heat were fireplaces and stoves.

Rubens' most important decorative commission came in 1621. It recalled an experience of twenty years earlier, when, in the entourage of the Duke of Mantua, he had attended the wedding in Florence of the young Medici princess, Marie, to Henry IV, King of France. Now Marie was the queen mother, Henry having been assassinated by a madman in 1610, and their son Louis having succeeded to the throne. In Paris Marie was building a magnificent palace for herself, called the Luxembourg, surrounded by extensive gardens that are now a popular public park. To satisfy her immense vanity and to try to win a place in history, she ordered Rubens to paint a series of twenty-one very large pictures glorifying her life and career.

The project challenged not only his imagination and artistic skills, but also his tact and diplomacy. The queen was a plain and rather dumpy woman approaching fifty, and, like many stupid people, was stubborn as well as vain. Rubens went to Paris and had long conversations with her. He made sketches and drawings, and arrived at a solution that completely satisfied Marie. The result is one of the finest examples of royal propaganda at this great scale. Resorting to Classical mythology and allegory, Rubens shows Juno, the queen of heaven, watching as the fates foretell Marie's illustrious future; Athena and Apollo educate her in arts and letters; while the Three Graces bestow upon her the gift of beauty. Heaven foreordains her marriage to Henry, and when, after her husband's death, she becomes the head of state, her rule is symbolically represented as equitable, peaceful, and enlightened. In truth it was just the opposite.

Everywhere in the superbly colorful canvases Rubens surrounds the queen with idealized gods and goddesses, handsome heroes, and beautiful ladies. The skies are filled with choruses of admiring cupids and attendant angels, and allegorical figures of such admirable qualities as virtue, justice, and wisdom. The queen's enemies, portrayed as cowering demons of repulsive ugliness, are put to flight by the overwhelming powers of righteousness. Even the squalid squabbles

Another painting from Rubens' series for Marie de' Medici pictures her coronation as queen of France and reveals the splendor of the seventeenth-century French court.

she had with her son, the young Louis XIII, which almost brought about a civil war and resulted in her banishment, are interpreted in a similarly heroic and flattering manner. Needless to say, the queen took the greatest interest in the progress of the pictures. When, in 1625, they were finally installed in a great hall of the Luxembourg Palace, she was delighted with the result. Today they are displayed in a large gallery of the Louvre, the artistic treasure house that is the national museum of France. On seeing them, one cannot but be filled with admiration at the splendor of their color, the abundance of fascinating detail, the sumptuousness of the costumes and settings, and feel the exuberance that the artist himself so obviously felt in their creation and execution. At the same time, we can recognize the extent of his extremely diplomatic interpretation of the events.

A similar series devoted to the far more estimable career of Henry IV, the queen's late husband, was never realized because of the tense political situation in France at the time. Rubens, after all, represented the Spanish Netherlands, a northern bastion of the immense power of the Hapsburgs who controlled much of Europe. Peter Paul was known to enjoy the trust of the archduke and the archduchess, and to have traveled in their service. So, though he was admired at the French court as an artist, and respected as a person, his political connections were regarded with suspicion. The queen undoubtedly wanted the project honoring the late king to be carried out, but her son's ministers held the purse strings, and the necessary funds were not forthcoming. The project never went beyond the few small sketches that Rubens had submitted for her approval.

During his visits to Paris, Peter Paul came to know Henrietta Maria, the queen's youngest child. A slender and attractive teenager with large, dark eyes, the princess was enchanted with the paintings of her mother's life, and became a friend and admirer of the artist. In 1625 he was a guest at her wedding to Charles I, the newly crowned King of England, just as he had been at her mother's marriage in Florence so many years before.

It was at the princess' wedding that Peter Paul met one of King Charles' closest friends, his chief advisor, the Duke of Buckingham. Like the king, the duke was a great admirer of art and an enthusiastic collector who was deeply impressed with Rubens' painting. He also respected him personally, and though he feared Spanish aggression in Europe, maintained a friendly relationship. They exchanged letters, and through the medium of the duke's agent, a countryman of Rubens named Balthasar Gerbier, Peter Paul advised on the acquisition of works of art for the duke's collection. Gerbier was an experienced courtier, a dealer in art and antiques, and a part-time miniature painter who had a keen eye for artistic quality, and a natural flair for scheming, spying, and general skullduggery. He was, therefore, very useful to the ambitious, impatient, and unscrupulous duke.

Rubens hoped that, because Buckingham was so close to the king, he might be won over to seek peace instead of war. But the duke's ill-advised attacks on Spain and other foreign misadventures kept Europe in turmoil and multiplied the young

After working as one of Rubens' assistants for some years, Anthony van Dyck was appointed court painter to Charles I of England. Here is his masterful King Charles at the Hunt, *of 1635.*

English king's international woes at the same time that an unruly Parliament with dangerously democratic ideas was undermining Charles' attempts at absolutist rule at home.

By the spring of 1628 the alliance of Spain and France against England had

In Spain Rubens met Diego Velázquez, the newly appointed court painter by Philip IV. Velázquez completed this dramatic portrait of his royal patron in 1635.

worn thin. Philip IV, the Spanish king, began seriously to reconsider the elaborate international agreements by which he hoped to advance his country's and the Catholic cause. As an expert on British affairs because of his contacts with Buckingham and his knowledge of the English court, Peter Paul was called to Madrid to confer. While he was there, Philip received the news that in the summer of 1628 Buckingham had been removed by assassination from the political scene, to which he had contributed little but disorder. For more than six months Philip and his advisors delayed making any decision as to what should be done next. While they procrastinated, Rubens made the most of his time by painting portraits of various members of the royal family for the Archduchess Isabella, who had never seen most of them, including her nephew the king.

He also met for the first time the young artist named Velázquez, who had just been appointed painter to the king. Velázquez was not yet thirty, a generation younger than Peter Paul, who had passed fifty, but Rubens saw the extraordinary quality of his work. The two artists came to know one another well as together they studied the many masterpieces in the extraordinarily rich royal collections. At Rubens' advice, the king sent Velázquez to Italy to enjoy the experience that Peter Paul had found essential for his own artistic career.

Finally, the king and his ministers made up their minds. They decided to sound out King Charles regarding peace with Spain. Rubens would be sent as ambassador. But with typical deviousness, Philip determined that Peter Paul would go, not as an emissary from Spain, but representing the Archduchess Isabella, the regent of the Spanish Netherlands. Rubens was by birth a gentleman, but because he worked with his hands as a painter, Philip could not consider him a suitable envoy direct from the Spanish court. Such an elevated responsibility could properly be undertaken only by a nobleman of august and ancient lineage. To give Rubens added cachet, however, the king gave him the meaningless title of Secretary to the Royal Council. Peter Paul set off at once to Brussels to confer with the archduchess. Then, after visiting his family briefly on the way, he boarded a ship at Antwerp to sail to London.

THE PURSUIT OF PEACE

Though Rubens' artistic and diplomatic career flourished during these years of uneasy alliances, war, and threats of war, his personal life had been painfully disrupted. In the summer of 1626, his beloved wife, Isabella, had died, totally unexpectedly. She had been only in her middle thirties, a happy, healthy young woman. The suddenness of her death made it even more shocking. Furthermore, it came barely three years after she and Rubens lost their only daughter, Clara Serena, who was not yet thirteen. The two boys, Albert and Nicholas, were twelve and eight years old at the time of their mother's death. Fortunately, there were a number of close and concerned relatives to help look after them. But Peter Paul was heartbroken. He adored his children, but Isabella had been the center of his life, and he was desolate without her.

There is no record of any possible cause for such an inexplicable tragedy, though it may have been due to an outbreak of the plague that occurred in Antwerp that summer. Rubens had been working on the huge painting above the

Charles I of England commissioned Rubens to decorate the ceiling of his Royal Banqueting House in London in 1630. The paintings (seen in detail opposite and on page 74) celebrate the reign of Charles' father, James I.

74

main altar of the cathedral, in which his earlier *Deposition* and *Elevation of the Cross* occupied either end of the crossing. His subject was the *Assumption of the Virgin,* the ascent of Mary to heaven after her death. Seen from a very low viewpoint, the event takes on an added drama as the figure of the Virgin rises buoyantly, with a host of fluttering and hovering angels greeting her from above. Below, the astonished apostles watch her miraculous ascent, while roses magically fill the empty tomb. Despite his sorrow, Rubens went resolutely back to work.

Because of Isabella's death, Rubens welcomed the interruption of the royal summons to Madrid and the voyage to England. As he wrote from London to a friend in August, 1629, he was filled with admiration for "the incredible wealth of excellent pictures, sculptures, and antique inscriptions to be seen" in the royal collections. Among the pictures were many from Mantua that Peter Paul knew well, that the spendthrift duke had been forced to sell to try to repair his finances. Rubens also found congenial companionship with British scholars who shared his interest in the Classical past, in the arts, architecture, and literature. He enjoyed the "beauty of the countryside, the charm of the people, and the magnificence and splendor of their . . . culture." He also observed, however, that the nobility live in such luxury that they are all in debt, and were thus vulnerable to the financial influence of the unscrupulous French ambassador. In spite of French plots and the machinations of the Venetian and Dutch ministers, Rubens had cordial conversations with King Charles, and managed to lay the foundations for a treaty of peace between England and Spain. In gratitude he was knighted by the king and awarded an honorary degree by the University of Cambridge.

During their conferences, Charles had been impressed by Rubens' courtesy and straightforwardness, in marked contrast to the arrogance and deceit of the French ambassador. The king came to regard him as an honored friend, whose character and ability he much admired, whose judgment he valued, and whose conversation he enjoyed. Rubens was one of the few who saw beyond the king's shyness and natural reserve to recognize him as a dedicated and idealistic man, who respected intelligence and had a strong sense of duty. He also noted that Charles had the most sophisticated appreciation for the arts "of any royal personage in Europe." Rubens also shared Charles' belief in the divine right of kings to enjoy personal and absolute rule. He himself faithfully served, in the Spanish monarchs

Rubens' daughter, Clara Serena, painted by her father in about 1618, died when she was only twelve years old.

Rubens painted his two sons, Albert and Nicholas, in about 1625.

and the regents of the Netherlands, sovereigns whose reigns were based on the same belief. But in the case of Charles, his near-fanatical adherence to this principle, which he had inherited from his father, James I, brought about increasing discord with Parliament, and eventually civil war, a temporary end to the monarchy, and after a disrupted and troubled reign, Charles' own martyrdom in 1649.

That was all in the future, however, and when Peter Paul sailed back to Antwerp, he took with him not only his new honors and valuable presents from the king, but also a commission he had much desired. After a friendly discussion, he and the king agreed that, for the sum of 3,000 pounds sterling, he was to decorate the immense ceiling of the Royal Banqueting House in London. Designed by the famous English architect Inigo Jones, the building was then nearing completion. The handsome interior is two stories high, and surrounded at the second floor level by a gallery. The hall, planned for court receptions, plays, balls, and musical performances, was large enough to contain an entire tennis court with space to spare.

The subject of the decorative scheme was to be the highlights of the reign of Charles' father, James I, the Scotsman who was the first of the Stuarts to occupy the English as well as the Scottish throne. James had not been a particularly distinguished monarch, but for an artist who could make a visual spectacle out of the questionable career of Marie de' Medici, it presented no difficulties. As Peter Paul sailed back across the English Channel to Antwerp, he was already designing it in his imagination.

The ceiling—one hundred ten feet long and fifty-five feet wide—is divided by ornate white and gold moldings into nine panels, five oval and four rectangular. The proportions of the hall are so perfectly calculated that its actual dimensions come as a surprise. The central oval, which shows the king, surrounded by angels and about to receive a laurel crown in heavenly recognition of his lifetime accomplishments, measures thirty-two by twenty-two and a half feet. Though in life King James was small and slender, Rubens makes him a heroic figure, and interprets the various episodes of his life with liveliness and verve. One scarcely notices the subjects for the vigorous spirit that the whole ceiling conveys.

The variety of rich color and contrasts of light and shade stand in marked contrast to the stately, static classicism of Inigo Jones' serene architecture. When the nine huge canvases were finally set in place in 1635, King Charles was delighted. The ceiling is one of the most splendid memorials to a historical figure, who, ironically, if he is remembered at all today, is known rather for his crusade against smoking tobacco than for his statesmanship.

On his return to Antwerp, Rubens was relieved to be able to take up the routine of daily family life again, with long hours of work with pupils and assistants in the studio. He was soon flooded with other commissions beside that for the Banqueting House ceiling. Albert and Nicholas were lively teenagers, and Peter Paul delighted in their company and that of friends and relatives. Among the latter was a young woman whom he had known since she was born, and had used as a model in some of his paintings. She was Hélène Fourment, the daughter of the sister of his late wife, Isabella. In 1630 they were married. It was not as a stranger that she entered the Rubens household, but as a close and dear friend, and she soon became the happy center of it.

Though it seems incongruous to us today, the bride was only sixteen, while Peter Paul was fifty-three. In those days it was not so unusual. Life was far shorter than today, people matured earlier, and such marriages were not uncommon. Many women died young because of complications of childbirth, just as many children did not live beyond infancy. Marriage in those days was more of a social institution than emotional choice of a mate. But Hélène proved to be as perfect a wife as Isabella had been. She respected Peter Paul's devotion to his first wife and honored him for it. She named her little daughter Isabella after her, adding her own name, to commemorate their affectionate relationship.

Rubens' family life was newly stabilized, but conditions in Europe were still chaotic. The Archduchess Isabella relied heavily in these times on Rubens' judgment and advice on the foreign affairs of the Spanish Netherlands. He was frequently called to Brussels to confer with her and her ministers. But the

Rubens never quite finished this portrait of his second wife, Hélène, with her children, Franz and Clara.

*In his later years Rubens turned increasingly to painting landscapes,
especially of the fertile countryside near his château, Het Steen.*

Archduchess Isabella became increasingly exhausted by the responsibilities of ruling alone since the death of Archduke Albert in 1621, and she became ill and died in 1633. Because of her wholehearted dedication to the welfare of the Spanish Netherlands, Rubens had been totally loyal to the archduchess. He was her valued advisor, and, during her later years, her trusted friend. He genuinely mourned her passing, and recognized that it marked the end of a chapter, not only in the history of the Netherlands, but also in his own life. It gave him a welcome freedom from the responsibilities of diplomacy and of being constantly on call as a chief advisor to the regent. And it gave him the opportunity to turn his entire attention to his family and to his art. He was fifty-six, and occasional attacks of what he called gout but was probably arthritis began to interfere from time to time with his painting, and reminded him of his advancing years. However, he pursued his art and his life as vigorously as ever.

Rubens' successful career made him a wealthy man and won him an international reputation as an artist. But he was also famous for, as King Charles had stated, "the services he has rendered . . . his rare devotion to his own sovereign, and the skill with which he has worked to restore a good understanding between the crowns of England and Spain." He kept up his international friendships by delightful personal and informative letters written in several languages. He took up collecting art and antiquities again, something he had given up after the death of his first wife. And he encouraged his older son, Albert, in his interest in Classical studies, which eventually led to his becoming an expert on Roman coinage. Late in the fall of 1635 he bought a large property in the country, roughly equidistant from Antwerp and Brussels.

The château Het Steen

The estate consisted of a château known as Het Steen and a number of other buildings, including a farm with barns, stables, and sheds, a large garden and orchard, and an ancient stone tower, all surrounded by a moat. The château and its outbuildings lie in the midst of the flat, fertile Flemish countryside, with cultivated fields, pastures dotted with cattle, and winding streams bordered by willows.

Though Rubens lived in strife-filled times, his life was dedicated to the arts of peace, to painting, scholarship, literature, friendship, family, and the appreciation of the beauty of the natural world. His diplomatic career had been devoted to a continuing search for peace. So the tranquil scenes around Het Steen must have meant a great deal to him. He spent much of his time at work, uninterrupted by the bustle of the city and the unexpected visitors who constantly sought him out in Antwerp. He also took time to ride through the country lanes that joined farms and hamlets, and made hundreds of sketches in the open air. Some of the details thus noted were later included in paintings. Others he recorded for his own pleasure.

Among many studies of nature that Rubens made near Het Steen is this Landscape with a Fallen Tree.

These drawings are full of light and air. They are swift, sure, and allusive, containing only just enough of what he saw to impart its flavor and suggest its atmosphere, and incomplete enough to engage one's imagination. The spacious landscapes that he began to paint at Het Steen during his later years grew out of such drawings. They recalled to his mind's eye the familiar scenes, enlivened by the play of light and shade that expresses both the time of the year as well as of the day. They reflect the constant variability of the limitless skies of the Netherlands. He painted different views of the château and the farm buildings, and included the old stone tower in a number of atmospheric pictures in the fading light of evening, or beneath stormy skies with threatening masses of dark clouds.

The extraordinary freedom and sweep of these airy landscapes to which Rubens turned in his later years were an inspiration to the generations of painters that came after him, when landscape became a major subject for artists.

After the death of the Archduchess Isabella in 1633, Philip IV of Spain appointed his younger brother Ferdinand as Regent of the Spanish Netherlands. Ferdinand had been made a cardinal by the pope while still a boy, as was often the case in those times with princes of dynasties loyal to the papacy. By this time Ferdinand was twenty-five years old, a vigorous and ambitious man with aspirations to a military career despite being a cardinal. And fate gave him an opportunity to prove himself. In the endless skirmishes and battles that have been called the Thirty Years' War, things had recently been going badly for the Hapsburgs, who had just suffered a humiliating defeat by an army of Swedes, Germans, and others. The timing was just right for Ferdinand. With Spanish troops accompanying him, he joined forces with the defeated army of his cousin, the King of Hungary, and mounted a successful counterattack. In April 1635, when Ferdinand reached the Netherlands, he came as a conquering hero.

The magistrates of Antwerp naturally turned to Rubens to take charge of the decorations to celebrate Ferdinand's official entry into the city. Time was short, but, as had been the case when the Archduke Albert and the Archduchess Isabella were welcomed thirty-six years before, all the artists of Antwerp were mobilized. Rubens designed the series of triumphal arches and other adornments of the route that the regent and his troops would follow. So important did the city fathers regard Peter Paul's designs that they had them engraved by one of his assistants and published with an account of the event by the official historian of Antwerp.

The subjects of these decorations were essentially political. They were intended to exalt the Hapsburg dynasty, to present Cardinal Ferdinand as an ideal, enlightened ruler, and also to inform him of the sorry condition of the city and of the Spanish Netherlands in general. Rubens finished the designs in about two weeks. The arches, colonnades, and trophies were constructed of canvas mounted on light wooden frames, and all of Antwerp's artists worked together to paint the architectural and sculptural details of Peter Paul's drawings. It is no surprise

Another of Rubens' sketches for Philip IV's hunting lodge, Battle of Giants and Titans, *clearly shows the influence of Guilio Romano (see page 31).*

In 1636 Philip IV of Spain asked Rubens to paint a series of pictures based on the work of the Roman poet Ovid to decorate a hunting lodge. This oil sketch, Cupid Riding a Dolphin, *shows Rubens' free, fluid style.*

that, with his famous speed and dexterity, Rubens accomplished a lion's share of the work. The result, however, was that he got an attack of the gout that kept him at home during the ceremonies of greeting. There the new regent called on him to inquire for his health and express his gratitude. The two had known one another since Peter Paul had met the newly appointed cardinal as a boy in Spain many years earlier. Ferdinand was well aware of the valuable diplomatic services Rubens had performed for the Spanish crown over the years, and admired him not only for his preeminence in the arts, but also for his spirit and character.

Ferdinand proved to be a vigorous and able governor. He defeated a combined attack of the Dutch and the French, who simultaneously launched assaults from the north and the south. This unexpected victory brought about a respite from the war that had dragged on for so long. Gradually the country began to prosper.

In 1636 Rubens received word from Cardinal Ferdinand that his brother, the king, had a commission for him. Philip was building a twenty-five room hunting lodge, called the Torre de la Parada, a few miles outside Madrid, and wanted it to be decorated throughout with scenes from Classical mythology, especially those described in the *Metamorphoses* by Ovid. (Metamorphoses means changes or transformations in Latin; Ovid was a Roman poet who wrote around the beginning of the Christian era.) Peter Paul was delighted. All his life he had been studying the world of antiquity, its literature, history, and art. Ovid's verses, which he had known since boyhood, had supplied subjects for painters and sculptors throughout the ages. They appeared on gems, cameos, coins, and medals, and in the works of Titian, Tintoretto, and the other artists of the Renaissance whom he had studied and admired. He started immediately to paint fluid oil sketches of the series of images and scenes that filled his mind as he recalled the familiar and colorful legends.

He completed panel after panel filled with gods and goddesses, centaurs and satyrs, nymphs and monsters. His swiftness and sureness of touch are amazing. They go beyond mere virtuosity to express, perhaps more completely than any other group of his works, the wonderful joy and vigor that informed his entire life and career. One would never guess from seeing them that the arthritis, or gout as he called it, that had troubled him from time to time, was now causing severe pain, and often crippled his right hand and arm so that he could not hold a pen or brush.

Despite this, in a year and a half he produced one hundred and twelve superb oil sketches. Such was the admiration and affection in which he was held by his colleagues, that he could call on several of the best painters in Antwerp to assist in producing the full-sized canvases from the sketches, much as they had worked together to create the decorations to welcome the regency of Ferdinand a few years before. In March, 1638, one hundred and twelve completed paintings were shipped to Spain. The king was so pleased with them that he immediately asked for more.

Similar to Rubens' marriage portrait with Isabella Brant (see page 45) is this etching by Rembrandt, the great Dutch painter of the next generation. Rembrandt's beloved wife, Saskia, poses with him.

But the series was never to be completed. During the cold and damp of the winter of 1638–39, Rubens' arthritis flared so critically and his general condition was so affected that at one point the doctors feared for his life. But he made an almost miraculous recovery, and was soon back in his studio. By early summer he had finished eighteen more sketches for King Philip. By fall there were four large canvases of Classical subjects on easels in his studio in various states of completion, also destined for Madrid. During the winter, however, the arthritis grew worse. He kept up his correspondence,

When Rubens painted this self-portrait, about 1640, he was in his early sixties. The glove on his right hand may hide the effects of the arthritis that plagued his later years.

though he had to dictate his letters. One would never suspect from reading them that he was ill because they are full of lively interest and affection.

In February, 1640, he heard from Italy that he had been elected an honorary member of the prestigious Academy of St. Luke in Rome. He remained hard at work in his studio, supervising students and assistants, and working when he could on several paintings. His mind was full of ideas for fulfilling other commissions that awaited his attention. But on the last day of May, the arthritis again flared, perhaps inducing the heart failure from which he suddenly died. Cardinal Ferdinand dispatched his own doctors from the regent's court in Brussels. They arrived the same day, but were already too late.

The news of Rubens' death spread quickly throughout the city and the rest of the Netherlands, as well as to Paris, Rome, Madrid, and London. He was mourned by patrons, friends, and fellow artists everywhere. Among the mourners was a young admirer, a Dutchman in his early thirties named Rembrandt, who was beginning to establish a reputation. His is the one name that stands along with Rubens' as the greatest of the Northern artists of the Baroque era. It was apparently through the circumstances of his being so much younger that Rembrandt was one of the few Netherlandish artists of the period that Rubens seems never to have met.

Hundreds of masses were celebrated in Peter Paul's memory throughout the Netherlands. He was buried in St. Jacques in Antwerp, the family's parish church. There, following his wishes, his widow, Hélène, had a memorial chapel constructed. The sculptured altar reflects the architectural style of his studio, and was probably, at least in part, designed by him and carried out by a pupil. Above the altar is one of Rubens' last paintings, a *Madonna and Child with Saints*. Tradition has it that the Virgin is a portrait of Hélène, and the Christ Child a likeness of his own youngest son, who was only three when Peter Paul died. The Mary Magdalene in the picture is thought to be a portrait of his first wife, Isabella; the St. Jerome, that of his late father; and the St. George, himself.

Whether these traditional identifications are correct or not, the ideal types of the women here, as in so many of his paintings, are based on likenesses of his wives and their female relatives. The picture has a gentle dignity. It is the work of a devout and devoted man, secure within himself, and happy in his family and with his life.

There have been few artists in history whose work was so widely known and admired during their lifetimes as was that of Peter Paul Rubens. He was unique in his combination of a distinguished diplomatic career with a prodigious artistic achievement that has been called "the most fertile in the history of painting." He was virtually the creator of the mature Baroque style, whose work dominated his own period and influenced and inspired generations of artists, even into the nineteenth century.

Everything Rubens did, from the briefest sketch to the most finished canvas, bears the mark of his vigorous and energetic personality. His compositions are full of movement, and tend to spiral in space with a force that seems to project beyond the limits of the picture. The vocabulary of forms that he created is unmatched in its variety and in expressing the vitality of nature. His art, like his life, reflects his enjoyment of the wonders of this world and of his belief in the greater wonders of a world to come.

Tradition has it that Rubens' painting for the family chapel includes portraits of himself and his family.

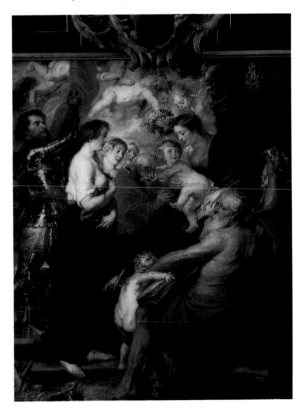

LIST OF ILLUSTRATIONS

PAGE 56: *Lion Hunt.* 1617–18. Oil on canvas, 98 x 148". Alte Pinakothek, Munich

PAGE 59: *Laocoön.* c. 150 B.C. Marble, height: 7'. Vatican Museums, Rome

PAGE 60: *Queen Tomyris with the Head of Cyrus.* 1615–18. Oil on canvas, 80½ x 141". Courtesy, Museum of Fine Arts, Boston. Juliana Cheney Edwards Collection

PAGE 64: *Marriage by Proxy of Marie de'Medici.* 1622–23. Oil on canvas, 155 1/16 x 116⅛". The Louvre, Paris

PAGE 67: *Coronation of Marie.* 155⅛ x 286¼". The Louvre, Paris

PAGE 69: Van Dyck. *Portrait of Charles I Hunting.* c. 1635. Oil on canvas, 8' 11" x 6' 11½". The Louvre, Paris

PAGE 70: Velázquez. *Portrait of Philip IV.* 1634–35. Oil on canvas, 9' 10½" x 10' 3⅝". The Prado, Madrid

PAGES 73, 74: Whitehall Banqueting Ceiling, London. 1632–34. Oil on 9 canvases, 110' x 55' 6" overall. British Crown Copyright. Reproduced with the permission of the Controller of Her Britannic Majesty's Stationery Office

PAGE 76: *Portrait of Clara Serena Rubens.* c. 1616. Canvas on panel, 13¼ x 10⅝". Collections of the Prince of Liechtenstein, Vaduz Castle

PAGE 77: *Portrait of the Artist's Sons (Albrecht and Nikolaus).* c. 1626. Oil on panel, 62¼ x 36¼". Collections of the Prince of Liechtenstein, Vaduz Castle

PAGE 79: *Hélène with Two Children.* 1635–38. Oil on panel, 44½ x 32¼". The Louvre, Paris

PAGE 80: *Landscape with a View of Steen.* 1636. Oil on panel, 53 x 93". The National Gallery, London

PAGE 81: The Château Het Steen. Photograph by Eddy van der Veen

PAGE 82: *Landscape with a Fallen Tree.* c. 1616. Chalk and pen and ink on paper, 22⅞ x 19¼". The Louvre, Paris

PAGE 84: *Battle of Giants and Titans (The Fall of the Titans).* 1637–38. Oil on panel, 10½ x 16¾". Musées Royaux des Beaux-Arts de Belgique, Brussels

PAGE 85: *Cupid Riding a Dolphin.* Oil on panel, 5 11/16 x 5 5/16". Musées Royaux des Beaux-Arts de Belgique, Brussels

PAGE 86: Rembrandt. *Rembrandt and His Wife Saskia.* 1636. Etching, 4⅛ x 3¾". The Pierpont Morgan Library, New York. B. 19i

PAGE 87: *Late Self-Portrait.* 1638–40. Oil on canvas, 43 x 33½". Kunsthistorisches Museum, Vienna

PAGE 89: *Madonna and Child with Saints.* 1638–40. Oil on panel, 83 x 76¾". Saint Jacob's Church, Antwerp

PHOTO CREDITS: pp. 1, 57: Copyright The British Museum, London; p. 6: A. Szenczi Maria, 1994; p. 9: Copyright A.C.L., Brussels; pp. 10, 24, 70: ORONOZ, Madrid; p. 20: Cameraphoto, Venice; pp. 22, 30: Canali; p. 26: Brunzel; pp. 29, 45, 54, 56: Artothek, Munich; pp. 31, 38–41: SCALA/Art Resource, New York; pp. 35–37, 84, 85: Copyright Institut Royal du Patrimoine Artistique (IRPA-KIK), Brussels; p. 46: Mario Quattrone, Florence; pp. 48, 49, 81: Eddy van der Veen; p. 59: Fototeca Unione, Rome; pp. 64, 67, 69, 79, 82: R.M.N., Paris; pp. 73, 74: Departments of the Environment and Transport, London; p. 89: Georges Van Pelt, Antwerp.

INDEX